BRAINY SCIENCE READERS

DO YOU KNOW ROCKET SCIENCE?

BE A **STEM** SUPERSTAR!

#1 SCIENCE AUTHOR FOR KIDS
Chris Ferrie

sourcebooks
eXplore

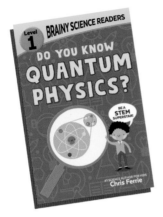

ALSO AVAILABLE

Text © 2021, 2022 by Chris Ferrie
Text adapted by Brooke Vitale
Illustrations by Chris Ferrie and Lindsay Dale-Scott
Cover and internal design © 2022 by Sourcebooks

All art was created digitally.

Published by Sourcebooks eXplore, an imprint of Sourcebooks Kids
P.O. Box 4410, Naperville, Illinois 60567–4410
(630) 961-3900
sourcebookskids.com

This product conforms to all applicable CPSC and CPSIA standards.

Cataloging-in-Publication Data is on file with the Library of Congress.

Source of Production: Wing King Tong Paper Products Co.
Ltd., Shenzhen, Guangdong Province, China
Date of Production: May 2022
Run Number: 5025964

Printed and bound in China.
WKT 10 9 8 7 6 5 4 3 2 1

Level

1

Dear Grown-up:

Welcome to the wonderful world of Brainy Science! Our mission is to help kids take their first steps to becoming independent readers! BRAINY SCIENCE will improve reading skills while immersing children into scientific theory. So blast off with BRAINY SCIENCE and observe as your budding scientist learns to READ and draw their own conclusions!

The Brainy Reading Method

Level 1: Beginner Reader
Pre K-Grade 1
Easy vocabulary. Short sentences. Word repetition. Simple content and stories. Correlation between art and text.

Level 2: Emerging Reader
Kindergarten-Grade 2
Letter blends. Compound sentences. Contractions.
Simple, high-interest storylines. Art offers visual cues to decipher text.

Level 3: Reading Alone
Grade 1-Grade 3
Longer, more complex storylines. Story told in paragraph form. Character development. More challenging letter blends and multisyllable words. Art enhances the story.

Hi there, big thinker.
Are you ready to learn?

KATHERINE JOHNSON

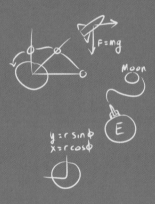

Today we will talk about Rocket Science.

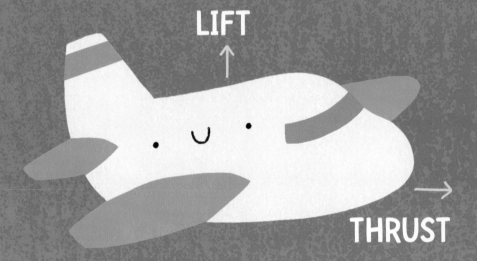

LIFT

THRUST

We will learn about
thrust and lift.
We will learn about
wings and tails.

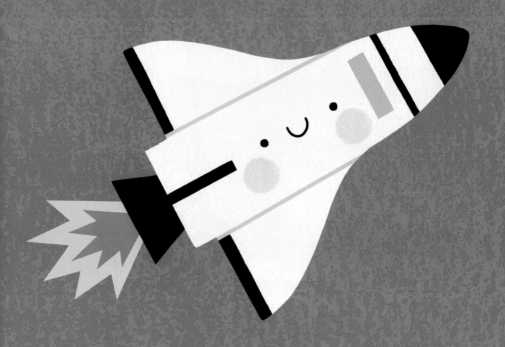

We will learn about
rocket ships!
Are you ready?
Let us begin.

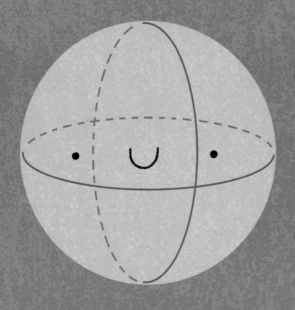

This is a ball.
The ball can bounce.

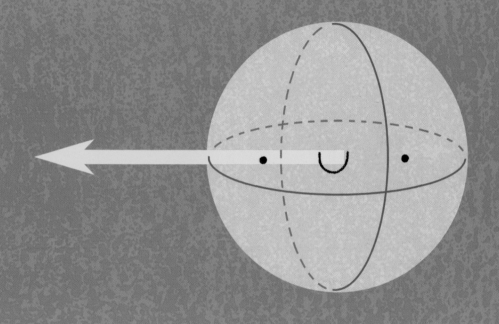

The ball can roll.
The ball passes through the air.

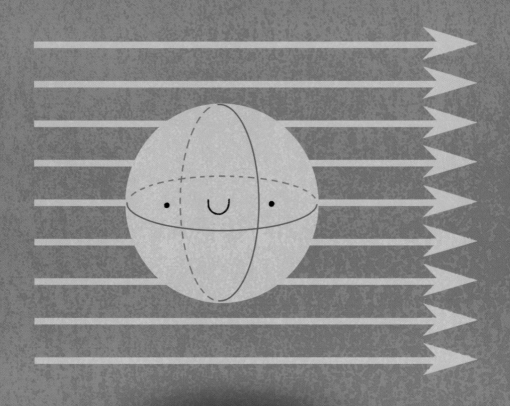

But air cannot pass
through the ball.
The ball is a solid object.

The air goes above the ball.
The air goes under the ball.
The air goes around the ball.

The air always goes around
the ball in the same way.
But what if the ball
was a different shape?

Now the ball is different.
Air still cannot go through it.
But air goes around it
in a different way.

What if the shape was turned?
What would happen to the air?

Tip the shape up.
The air goes up.

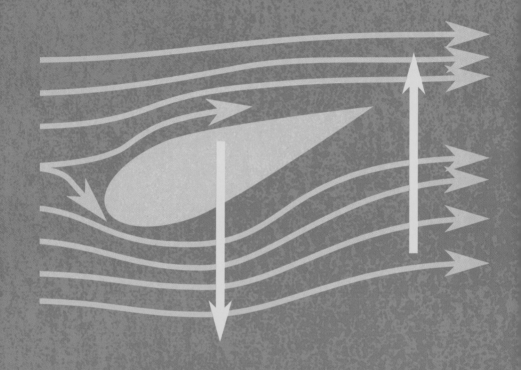

If the air goes up,
the shape goes down.

Tip the shape down.
The air goes down.

If the air goes down,
the shape goes up.

The force that pushes the shape up is called lift.

Gravity pulls the shape down. The force that pulls the shape down is called weight.

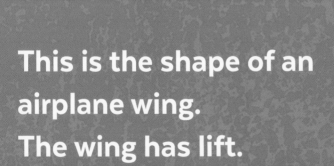

This is the shape of an
airplane wing.
The wing has lift.

But the wing cannot move
on its own.
How do we make the
wing move?

We put it on something
that can move.
We put it on a rocket ship.

This is a rocket ship.
It does not have one wing.
It has two wings!

The rocket ship cannot move
on its own.
It needs power.
The power comes from gas.

The gas makes the ship go.
It comes out of the ship.

The force of the gas coming out
makes the ship move forward.

The faster the gas goes,
the faster the ship goes.

The gas comes out the fastest
when it is on fire.
So, we make it explode!

The ship moves forward.
The force that pushes it
is called thrust.

Lift pushes the ship up.
Thrust pushes the ship forward.
With lift and thrust
we can go to the moon!

Good job, big thinker.

Now you know
ROCKET
SCIENCE!